The Lonely Year

John Del Giudice

ISBN: 098940840X
ISBN-13: 978-0989408400

The Lonely Year

FeatherStone Press

I have a great deal of company in my house;
especially in the morning, when nobody calls.

~Henry David Thoreau

CONTENTS

An Introduction

I

Here I stand at thirty-three,

    ready to begin.

To cast words, these worlds,

Into our spoken existence.

From childhood memories,

I, skipping along the treetops,

Balancing on branches

    just barely new.

Searching for blue rocks in a creek

(I'm certain of an apple tree, too).

I fell from a rural isolation,

And landed in the city's obscurity.

There was a Woolworth,

Which my grandmother called

    the Five and Dime.

Along the street, from the lampposts,

They hung decorations at Christmas time.

At some point I latched a lock

    to a ladder rung.

II

It was the summer when,

I found myself in isolation

    again,

On a half-dirt, half-paved road.

This was not where I was born,

Nor my parents, or their parents;

(I was convinced no one lived here).

I spoke with an un-aged authority,

Which confounded the parents

    of my peers.

Their minds were sordid and crude;

I was the voice of one crying

    in the wilderness.

I walked the forest paths,

And held nature's deepest hues,

Obscured by tree, bush, and canopy.

I hid from society's need to conform.

III

Asleep at night I had a vision:

I stood in front of hundreds

   gathered to listen,

And spoke the same words which

   I wrote before.

To draw a line, create discord, and

   cause a division.

But the utterance fell at inception, merely

   littering the floor.

I looked and also beheld:

Sundry letters slowly falling like flakes

   of feathery snow,

Which hit the ground and formed

   creation here below,

Clumped together words comprising

   everything we see,

"Write," I heard, and then the word

       was handed thus to me.

I waited countless nights in

       despair for this,

       my work to begin.

Watching the sway of the

       barren maple branches.

I now hear the palm fronds

       gently clap and hiss,

And the lilies both toil and spin.

IV

I steered a rudderless ship

And jumped into the sea;

Then, floating on my back,

I drifted home to me.

V

I looked for you beyond

    the drooling dead.

And there you stood—

Legs lustered by lampshade light.

You are my sign of adoration:

The signifier and the signified.

Why do we make so much of this?

    In the end,

It's just legs and arms and heads.

What of these is so complex?

Simply bare limbs over naked threads.

Who knows what happened to us?

To what do we attribute each disaster?

Which are accelerating daily in this chaos.

This spinning world throws us into a whirlwind

Though this is not what we intend.

When you left I took a long bath.

I pulled the stopper and watched in wonder

The whirling, twirling water spinning with increasing speed

The closer it came to the end.

VI

For every tragedy we erect a monument,

Commemorating sorrow with a golden calf,

As if to say "forget the error and look to this;"

I'll look to a bronze snake on a pole instead.

I wanted to write a hundred years ago,

Before this present, wretched age

In which we stand bewildered by a billion lights

That misdirect the paths we seek.

Yet I was summoned and so I shall commence.

Almost against my will I perform this task,

This compulsory commission,

This endless blue rock searching.

VII

With childlike questioning we reason our love.

On a bed of leaves we speak

To the whispering audience in the canopy above;

The shared isolation we mutually seek.

You asked me about our love,

And I didn't have much to say:

It pauses, briefly, before continuing on its way.

VIII

Let us hide from our parents

And sneak into the woods

To be alone

Near the birch trees

Whose bark burns

So brilliantly:

Engulfed in flames

Enflamed in passion,

And lose ourselves.

IX

There is

An unseen parallel

To this life

In which actions

Are mirrored

And there we will meet again,

And yet for the first time

In those eternal fields.

The last time

We first met

We couldn't speak.

This time we shall

Meet as children

With equal curiosity

And wonder.

X

I cannot rely on the days of rest

Before I begin my work.

A deathbed would be ideal,

But that is seldom found.

I know that life is taken

While we try to live;

The pitcher cracks before the fountain,

And the wheel is broken at the well.

Repossession

The only time I was myself and truly alive

Was my life lived until about the age of five,

Before the schoolyard's geodesic dome;

Free to live in a world of my own creation,

Free to rely solely on my imagination

In the security of my mother's home.

Then I walked to school to stand in lines,

To be captured in the chain-link confines;

I still find this hard to understand.

Barred from daydreaming as they taught,

Barred from forming independent thought,

And placed in a seat to raise my hand.

I rushed home then, as I still do now

And continue with my self-made vow

To get back to my creativity.

Compelled to abandon in pursuit of gain,

Compelled to work for what I disdain:

One-third of the day in captivity.

This is the real self I leave behind each day,

The real self the world tries to wash away

Through a succession of subtle waves.

Imposed to erode myself from me,

Imposed to follow, yet set myself free

From the flickering shadows in the caves.

But I have not forgotten you, John,

Nor the floor you're still sitting upon,

Dressed in your sky blue shorts.

Caught in the stars through the ethereal ceiling,

Caught in a world through thoughts revealing

All the truth that wisdom distorts.

Your fort under the table is still intact

Though its walls have chipped and cracked,

I have come to find you only when,

Lost to a tattered nonentity,

Lost with a confused identity,

But come, let us dream again.

A Defensive Tree

Outside there is a tree with thorns

To protect itself from parasites.

Each barb serves to fend, and forewarns

Every fowl its fruit invites.

The tree stands undefiled,

And bares its armor bright.

No pest is betrayed or beguiled

When all the spikes are clear to sight.

But one day a bird descended

And perched like a prince alone.

It was not the branch that he befriended;

The tree itself became his throne.

I felt fortunate to witness this sight,

As if both forces dueled for me:

The bird, by perching, defended its right,

The branch, though thwarted, protected the tree.

Although now it sounds absurd,

I envied both the branch and bird

And still can't say what I'd rather be—

A defiant bird or a defensive tree.

Sincere Love

What more can I possibly do

To show my love and make it true?

Change the sea to a deeper blue?

Seize the stars and bring them to you?

Even if I could you'd have no need,

Wealth can't cause a heart to bleed.

Love is not born from selfish greed,

Nor wrought from any foolish deed.

Is love merely a practiced art?

Or a game in which we play a part?

Like Cupid with his magic dart

Who fires blindly and pierces the heart.

Instead of changing the tint of the sky

Or plotting to stop the sun passing by

I'll give to love of my heart's supply

And whatever it asks I will not deny.

A sincere love is what you deserve

So what purpose do possessions serve?

And who am I to not preserve

A law that all love must observe?

In spite of lies from bards of old

Of all the actions done or told

The hardest, rarest, and one most bold

Is to give another your heart to hold.

The Spider

I watched a spider crawl

Into the corner of my room,

Then I went into the kitchen

For to fetch my wooden broom.

When I returned I found it

Scurrying across the floor,

Preferring instead to build its web

In the upper corner of my door.

I waited a little while

As it worked above my head,

I saw a world created

Pieced together thread by thread.

It then sat in the center

Of a universe all its own,

Autonomous and independent—

It survives by living alone.

Unable to withstand much more

I triumphantly raised the broom,

I destroyed the creature and its world

And expelled them from my room.

Spiders are indeed repulsive,

Yet for reasons not realized:

Any self-sufficient being

Must instinctually be despised.

Aeolian Harp

If fate cannot be thwarted, my love,

Then let it be our guide.

All our attempts to steer the course

Are but a blowing against the tide.

And though we lived, and loved, and laughed,

Unknown and miles away,

Our feet walked a circular path

That led us to this day.

And since this is the case, my love,

Since you and I are pinned,

To hear the song of our Aeolian harp

Let us point it toward the wind.

Note to Self

Either she loves you

And you will be together—

In which case you don't need to worry.

Or she does not love you

And you will not be together—

In which case you don't need to worry.

Auguries of Indolence

The sun knows to rise each day

And the earth is blessed by a single ray.

And if it did not shed its light

Then we would walk in endless night.

So why should we not also rise

And put off pleasure's false disguise?

By lying supinely on your back

All you have is all you lack.

How will your work commence

If you are shackled to your indolence?

Those of this world who sleep the best

Complete their work before they rest.

On what basis, then, can we dream?

When all of our goals we disesteem.

Whether your task is great or small

In whatever you do, give it your all.

Even the ant hoisting a grain

Works towards a purpose he must attain.

Every leaf on every tree

Binds to form the canopy,

And every single blade of grass

Forgives the foot that cut the path.

So get up, get up! The sun has almost set

On a million dreams not accomplished yet.

The Human Heart

The functions of the body

Belong to the brain,

And every action

Condescends thereto:

Binding memories in a dizzying domain,

Engendering sorrow from old cares renewed.

But there is another agent

Which threatens this reign,

And forces a perspective

From its own unique view.

Each to the other is held in disdain,

Each to the other discredits what's true.

Within a civil war life is sustained,

(Peace never reached between the two).

The mammalian mind is master

And ruler over every part,

Yet is disturbed by the delicate disaster,

Haunted by the human heart.

California

California has no seasons,

Save a long perpetual one;

The days change, the months go by,

And all under the same sun.

How can I be mournful

When every day is spring?

How can I feel joyful

With no solstice bells to ring?

Every plant is perennial

And placed in perfect rows,

And artificially nourished

By the water from a hose.

You can't enjoy a day of summer

And be thankful for a breeze

If you've never been so cold

You feared your blood would freeze.

The seasons create a cycle,

Wherein their significance lies,

But only one is needed

In the state where no one dies.

Artistic License

There are times when I long to be an artist

for I could never make you undress for me,

and lie exposed like a lonely tree in a barren field.

I could never make you disrobe

for the benefit of my pen—like an artist can;

with his outstretched hand like a pauper, begging.

Yet for an artist, with his exonerated pen,

you will sit silently, trying not to quiver and shake;
wondering

if his keen and perceptive eyes have unlocked your
concealed flaws:

the little blemishes and imperfections that only a lover
should ever see.

An artist is allowed into the sacred grounds of your
hallowed flesh,

and he alone is permitted to gaze at the fullness of your
breasts.

Free and uninhibited, your vulnerable, unveiled skin

is set before him plainly. While my useless, poetic pen

cannot reveal a simple shoulder, let alone your single flesh.

I must rely on invention, and picture you sitting there

with your eyes diverted to the corner of my room

patiently waiting for me to stop.

Yet, one advantage I have over the artist:

I can always summon you to my mind,

where your body is forever sprawled over my bed.

Only my words to capture your curves.

Only my words to fashion your frame.

Only my words to follow your features.

And I have only these to lean upon

when you're gone; to read and re-read

like a child finding comfort in his favorite book.

The artist's pen is exact and true;

his hand creates the accurate portrayal,

while the poet's only recourse is in hyperbolic expressions.

To be blessed with the byproducts of a skillful hand,

I'd abandon every letter and renounce my tongue.

The poet's curse is the eternal search of a template for his words.

The Pond

When at first I saw them

Perched on a rock by the edge of a pond,

I wondered how these two ducks

Came to live where no others dwelled.

A week had passed before I saw them again,

Both taking turns following each other.

How much better I thought, together here alone,

Lacking nothing by leaving the flock.

My love, let us find our pond.

Everything Falls Apart

Eventually everything falls apart,

Nothing is left of our love or hate;

It was designed that way from the start.

Like the innocence of a child's heart

Soon all will disintegrate;

Eventually everything falls apart.

We watch our possessions slowly depart

Obeying the course determined by fate;

It was designed that way from the start.

Time will not spare our precious art,

And nothing we have will compensate;

Eventually everything falls apart.

We see the senility of those once smart

Deprived of their prior state;

It was designed that way from the start.

Corrosion seeps in and follows its chart,

And all we can do is watch and wait.

Eventually everything falls apart—

It was designed that way from the start.

Giraffes

Mother, those jumping giraffes

With which you papered the walls of my childhood room

Were prophetic.

Their feet never touched the ground.

Perpetually suspended,

Forever falling;

Mother, I have become such as one.

Rising Sun

If asked to define our love

I wouldn't know what to say.

You see the rays of the rising sun

And then you know it's day.

How can I express in words

The sentiments of the heart?

Thoughts and feelings have never met

And should always be kept apart.

But if our love must be named

And ultimately defined thereby:

Then we are two solitary stars

Shining in the same night sky.

Travel

It doesn't matter where I go,

Or even if I go,

I have already left

Innumerable cares behind:

Scattered little notes on bubble gum wrapping,

Careless thoughts forever lost in eternal napping,

I have shed the proverbial skin,

Transfigured as sacrificial lamb,

But not the physical flesh,

And so I remain as I was—as I am.

Each night like a proselyte

I rehearse the creeds

That bid my…flight…

My…pilgrimage…

My…isolated retreat…

My…solitary confinement…

My…ultimate self-defeat.

And yet I see myself before me

Condemned without defense,

Summoned by a great command,

"Go thou East" and

"Forthwith go ye hence."

But where will I go

If I arrive there as me?

What are new places

Except new things to see?

En route to Damascus

Let my conversion be

Designed to uproot the

Branch laden tree

Not felled by persuasion,

But overtaken rapturously.

Yea, though I settle on

The far side of the sea,

I shall still see myself before me.

The Marriage Sin

At first we enjoy a little taste,

Then drunkenness begins.

Such is the case with all our follies—

The wickedness of our sins.

Violent thoughts stem from the heart

Where all evil deeds reside:

Wrath, pride, and covetousness,

Plus a million more beside.

A man who is a raging thief

Began with petty crimes.

What soon equates to large amounts

Began with nickels and dimes.

Sin is a slippery slope,

As a horse goes before the carriage;

And divorce is a grievous sin,

Preceded by the first, which is marriage.

Marigolds

I walked passed the marigolds today,

The ones you planted out back

Which no one sees

And yet their beauty is eternal.

They stand like royal sentries

In blood red and orange dress

For their own sake,

But I noticed them.

And this morning I called you marigold.

Reflection

Her love I, but fate deems

Nothing for us, leaving only

Longing and emptiness like

Resounding hollow bells

Vibrating waves of passions;

And despair engenders only

Resentment. Yet, embers burning

In hand, I grab fire flaming the coals,

The flaming fire grab I, hand in

Burning embers. Yet, resentment

Only engenders despair, and

Passions of waves vibrating bells,

Hollow, resounding like emptiness

And longing, only leaving us for nothing,

Deems fate…but I love her.

Kindergarten

I know the course you must go through,

It is the same garden in which we all grew,

And I would stand in your stead to save you.

To witness the seed that I have sown

Get replanted in a plot that is not my own

As a plant gets repotted when it has grown.

The innocence I cultivated with consistent care,

And laying the foundation for your castle in the air

Slowly unravels through inculcated delicate despair.

Thirty hands to act in one accord as the slayer,

As I am dealt the fated role of betrayer,

And merely perform in this passion as a player.

All past fears, doubts, and anxieties

Come streaming back in floods over me

As I stand inside your Gethsemane.

All things go along as planned; nothing amiss,

And before I depart, I gently plant a kiss

As I leave you in a forsaken state like this.

The hour has come; I stand apart on the grass

To gaze at you through the window of your class,

And how I desperately long to let this cup pass.

You are turned over to the authorities to guide—

To persecute your spirit and pierce your side,

To be crushed, and crippled, and crucified.

Over the years, they will slowly corrode and kill,

Yet this must be done, though this is not my will,

And I know this full well, for I bear the scars still.

Stigma

I wait for you,

My savior,

My nameless, faceless

Darling.

I have mortified the flesh

For you, beloved,

I have fashioned myself

A martyr.

Peace and rest, comfort

And love,

These the promised gifts

You swore.

I hold nothing in these

Stigmatic hands

Save the scars my patience

Bore.

"Wait," I'm told,

"There's some work to be done,"

And while you bask in your

Own sunlight;

It is to the wailing voices

Outside my window below

To which I lull myself to sleep

Each night.

A Poem at a Price

She told me that she hated poetry

With each palm flatly placed upon my chest

As she glided on top of me rhythmically;

The moon reflecting off the wet skin between her breasts.

A slight quiver detected as she silently came,

She simply got off, got up, and then got dressed.

I watched in breathless desire, as a burning flame,

While she left me lying quite still and bereft.

And she is one who can afford to hate poetry,

But as for me, it is all that I have left.

The Lonely Year

From end to end

I lingered in fall,

Sinking sorrows with

Tear-mixed alcohol.

I took an interest

In the falling leaves—

The exiled petals the

Branch never retrieves

In their wayward

Circling descent;

The tossing turmoil

Of the season spent.

Time is a healer,

But my wounds got worse.

The hands of the clock

Were set in reverse.

And every child's face

Brought me to tears—

So I turned my eyes

And blocked my ears.

My heart is stitched

From a continuous tear;

A patchwork of scraps—

Torn and threadbare.

The locked memories

Haunted my sleep,

Flashing moments

Plucked from a heap.

I stand still

Without a defense,

And nothing I connect

Seems to make sense:

The putting asunder,

The sacrificial knife.

The lonely year

Is one of a lonely life.

Beside Still Waters

Let me stand in his stead

where you have placed him as a god;

for I have heard your supplications.

Allow me to absolve

all your former transgressions,

that you may lie down in green pastures.

And seek no more

forgiveness in his eyes,

for in mine your heart is pure.

And I will lead you beside still waters.

I will prepare a table for you.

I will restore your soul.

From his abdicated throne

I will take up residence,

and you shall not be in want.

Leaf Raking

I was raking up the leaves one day

Where hundreds had hit the ground,

And when I had thought all the leaves were caught

I turned and more were found.

These same leaves once provided shade,

They once flourished in the sun,

Now they lie down, their green has turned brown,

Their course, once complete, is done.

And so my thoughts turned to the graves

Where many thousands lie;

Just as the leaves that float from the trees,

So too all men must die.

I stood on the lawn, a solitary reaper

Of all the leaves that fell;

I knew that in spring they'd return like a king,

Yet for the dead I could not tell.

But I know one day a hand will come

To claim these bodies too;

Though time has decayed what once danced and played,

They will be restored to a life brand new.

These leaves revive a truth,

And were made just for this reason:

That from their birth till they sleep in the earth

Everyone's life is a season.

The Stars

The bright stars

Are little diamond shards

When you're three feet tall,

But if your eyes

Were the night skies

The stars wouldn't matter at all.

A full moon

Is a white balloon

Drifting throughout the night,

It chases the sun,

And makes him run

To pour on earth its ethereal light.

A cloud in fall

Is a woolen shawl

Floating in a clear blue sea,

But many pass by

And never see the sky

Nor look beyond the height of a tree.

You can't see

What's so clear to me,

Why I gaze at you while you sleep,

To me you are

Every bright star,

You're the world and mine to keep.

Atlas Slave

A faceless man with indistinct features:

Half-entombed body missing hands and feet;

Hoisting on my shoulders an endless burden

That by these conditions I was made complete.

It was not that I was abandoned

And left a half-hewn marble block;

I am forever in the act of becoming—

Continually emerging from the rock.

And I know the Master's hand has crafted me

To exist, undefined, in frozen formation;

Not as a finished marble masterpiece,

But as a work in perpetual creation.

This and Only This

The years we spent together lovingly

Dissolved in duration as if a dream.

To see our moments like water droplets

That trickle away from love's shallow stream.

We slowly disappeared from each other,

Left starving from a passion underfed,

All while crossing each other daily

Under one roof, asleep in the same bed.

Our lives together, our pain and our love,

Paraded like a silent marching band.

With no monument to mark the passing—

Without a flag left waving in the sand.

Nothing will attest to the love we shared,

Only a poem to bear us witness

To a love that for us was real and yet,

This is all we have—this and only this.

To the Young

Though scorched by a vitriolic tongue,

And dangled over phantom fires to condemn,

The world ever belongs to the young

And everything made conspires for them.

They are scared from fear they don't understand,

Thinking the old are wise and learned,

But the keys of the kingdom are in their hand,

And given an inheritance not valued nor earned.

The old are prancing on a stage their elders made,

(Just as your teacher is only an actress).

The aged authorities merely masquerade,

They know no more than you, in fact less.

One day you will awaken to a different world

And stagger, confounded by being less sturdy

As if by force, you were violently hurled

Into the foreign eyes of one turned thirty.

You are only leased ownership for a time

And then you slip into utter obscurity;

Estranged from yourself in the days of your prime

While you trade freedom and passion for security.

Casting unheard votes in predetermined national elections,

Investments, portfolios, stocks in a 401k,

Alignment to absurd parties with dilettantish affections,

And mandatory morning meetings at 9:15 each day.

This must be counted along with all that's true:

You own the world when it does not own you.

We Laugh and Walk Away

It starts with a common greeting,

a subtle look with the eye,

then a casual conversation

before we say goodbye.

Nothing is expected,

we do not ask for more;

to hope for a future

seems rather premature.

So we talk about the weather,

trying hard not to display

any thoughts of affection;

then we laugh and walk away.

It starts on a single night

masked in moonlit mist;

every person we encounter

is complicit to our tryst.

Excited by expectations,

filled with fears to overcome;

we silently enjoy the thoughts

of what we may become.

So we end the evening drinking

in a dimly lit café,

we kiss each other nervously

and just laugh and walk away.

It starts with a routine:

a long monotonous chain;

we see each other daily

as our love turns to disdain.

Full of failed expectations,

that neither of us could meet,

our dissatisfaction becomes

our mutual defeat.

So we pass each other swiftly

as we prepare to start the day;

we kiss without emotion,

without a laugh we walk away.

It starts by slow resentment—

a severe, reproachful eye.

We pass each other silently

and leave with no goodbye.

With nothing more to expect,

all our secrets are revealed;

we hurt each other constantly

for the wounds that have not healed.

So finally we end it

as the leaves of love decay;

we give one final look behind

and then we laugh,

and walk away.

Memory

Our memory is a torturous game

When events from the past we are forced to reclaim.

It's heavily one-sided, which hardly seems fair

When our fondest memories are so short and so rare.

A single phrase that you may carelessly utter,

Is stored in my brain and adds to the clutter.

At night, while lying still on my bed,

It ricochets off the walls in my head.

From your hand that once rested in my lap,

I now bare the scars of a leg-hold trap.

It's not a poor memory that I lament,

It's having one too good that I resent.

The only consolation in this painful mess,

Is that you too may be fraught with distress.

And from all the love that we once shared,

May we both walk away a little impaired.

Definitions

We lie on the floor and create

A little private world;

We assign roles to your dolls.

I play the part of different characters,

While you laugh at their personalities—

And we call this "make-believe."

Then I am compelled to leave

And pretend in a pre-made story;

I am given a title that defines my role.

And there I act a different part,

While you wait for me to return—

And this we call "reality."

Future Token

We carve our names in wet cement,

And smear summer-melted tar with a broken stick.

The random act of a curious youth—

Accidental time capsules for our futures selves.

These become our mental deities

When they frustrate the eroding effects of time.

To which we can return years after and say,

"Look, here's the mark I left when I was a kid."

In these we meet ourselves again—

A minor victory in life's defeat.

The world consumes our ephemeral existence,

Absorbing us and all we thought would last.

Life is only scattered memories.

Our daily diary is the anthill

That some careless child tramples

On his way to build a future token.

Yet, in these signs we redeem ourselves,

And become the heroes of your own lives.

The immutable that time cannot decay

Lasts long enough to affirm a life once lived.

ABOUT THE AUTHOR

John Del Giudice is a writer and poet living in California. Spending his
early years living in different states on the east coast, his writings are a
delicate blend of city insouciance and rural sensibilities.
For more information visit www.johndelgiudice.com.

www.ingramcontent.com/pod-product-compliance
Lightning Source LLC
Chambersburg PA
CBHW031611040426
42452CB00006B/471